DRIVING LESSONS

A Father, a Son, and the Healing Power of Golf

STEVE FRIEDMAN

INTRODUCTION BY JAMES DODSON,
BESTSELLING AUTHOR
OF *Final Rounds*

RODALE.

Rodale books may be purchased for business or promotional use or for special sales. For information, please write to:

Special Markets Department, Rodale, Inc.,
733 Third Avenue, New York, NY 10017

Printed in the United States of America

Rodale Inc. makes every effort to use acid-free ♾, recycled paper ♻.

A portion of this book appeared originally in the May 2005 issue of
Travel + Leisure Golf.

Illustrations by Daniel Pelavin

Book design by Sara Stemen

Library of Congress Cataloging-in-Publication Data
Friedman, Steve.
    Driving lessons : a father, a son, and the healing power of golf / Steve Friedman.
        p.   cm.
    ISBN 978-1-60529-125-3 (hardback)
    1. Golf--Anecdotes.   2. Golfers--Family relationships.   3. Fathers and sons.
    4. Friedman, Steve.   I. Title.
GV967.F85   2011
796.352--dc22   2011003613

Distributed to the trade by Macmillan

2   4   6   8   10   9   7   5   3   1   hardcover

We inspire and enable people to improve their lives and the world around them.
www.rodalebooks.com

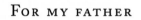

FOR MY FATHER

DRIVING LESSONS

Introduction

By James Dodson

⁂

LET me try to explain why Steve Friedman's lovely memoir *Driving Lessons* resonates so powerfully for me.

Back in the mid-'70s, during my senior year in college, I went home on several weekends to play a series of "friendly" father-son golf matches against my dad's friend Robert and Robert's grown son Rick.

On paper it seemed like a pretty appealing idea. After all, the two dads were good friends who had been playing together for more than a decade, and both sons were single-digit handicappers, though at that time I was hitting far more books than fairways.

"There's just one thing," my father pointed out before the first match. "Rick can be pretty intense, and his daddy never stops coaching him. I think Robert hoped Rick might be good enough to turn pro someday, but it never worked out." He added that Rick was good enough to play for a top Southern college but now worked for his old man, which sometimes explained the palpable tension between the two.

"Junior's a scratch player but he has a tendency to lose his cool. You just stay loose and we'll just be ourselves and find a way to handle them. It'll be fun. I'll buy the beer afterwards."

Truth be told, I came to dread these father-son team encounters. For one thing, the matches turned out to be short on fraternal bonhomie and long on repressed male anger and frustration, a walking seminar on youthful angst and paternal disappointment.

As I'd been warned, Robert never stopped giving Rick sharply worded advice on his swing path or his weight shift or his flying elbow or whatever, while the son brooded and lashed even harder at the ball, pounding it 300 yards down the seam, other times sending it to oblivion across adjoining fairways. More than once, at a key moment where he needed to pull off a good shot, Rick failed to do so and actually threw his club down in disgust.

In a perverse sort of way, this made the matches more satisfying for me than they might have been, for Robert and Rick's psychological dynamic was exactly the opposite of what existed between me and my old man. As usual, my dad and I walked along talking about everything from Nixon's foreign policy initiatives to the accursed growth of Day-Glo orange golf balls. (In these instances, my dad was enthusiastically pro, while I was stridently con.) As usual, we had a grand old time needling each other about these subjects and a million other things that made our golf sorties such a blast.

Somehow through it all, though I was something of a reformed club-thrower and competitive hothead myself, we almost always managed to find a way to beat Rick and his father by the slimmest of margins, which of course doubled their misery.

"You know," Rick said to me after losing the third and final match to us, "you wouldn't be a half bad player if you took this game seriously and learned to concentrate on it."

"You might be right," I was forced to agree, "but it wouldn't be half as much fun."

*

The simple truth is, I took up playing golf principally because I loved being around my funny, philosophical father, an upbeat character I took to calling (not entirely kindly) "Opti the Mystic" during my know-it-all teenage years, owing to his tendency to quote some ancient sage on faith or impermanence when you least expected it, and to find the silver lining in almost any situation. If it's true, as Carl Jung insists, that sons dream their father's dream, perhaps it was simply inevitable that I would fall for my old man's favorite game, which he fell in love with while stationed in Scotland near Lytham St. Annes during the Second World War.

Whatever else is true, golf is the most social game on earth, typically involving hours of walking and talking with playing companions and roughly only three minutes, give or take, of actual ball-striking concentration. In fact, that may help explain why a high percentage of people who take up the game and come to love it do so under the initial influence and guidance of a thoughtful parent, a golf-loving mom or dad who passes along something far more valuable than a few good swing tips.

Given the game's storied traditions of fair play and honest self-conduct, it's scarce wonder the auld game has descended from its woolly Scottish antecedents as a great teaching tool for life—and a splendid means for keeping the communication lines between generations open and active.

A decade or so ago, not long after I published an account of my early golf life with my dad in a memoir called *Final Rounds*, framing the tale in what turned out to be our first and last golf pilgrimage to England and Scotland, I began receiving amazing letters from readers eager to tell me about their own relationships with either their fathers or sons through the game of golf.

STEVE FRIEDMAN

Not all mirrored my experience of having a father who felt it was both sufficient and wise to simply introduce his son to the assorted pleasures and Darwinist charms of life's most difficult game and leave it at that— artfully igniting my passion, if you will, by simply revealing the joy and friendships the game provided. My dad's reluctance to ever show me anything more than a basic correct setup and swing—calmly pointing out that if I really wanted to improve my game I should either watch fine players or take lessons from our profane and crusty old pro—would have nicely done a Zen master proud. By offering me only a tantalizing glimpse of paradise, in effect, he guaranteed I would be a disciple of the game forever.

In fact, many of the moving and surprisingly detailed letters I received were from sons (and even a few daughters) who'd either not had the benefit of a golf-loving parent or perhaps had grown up without a father entirely—and were, as a result, extramotivated to be a terrific, supportive dad to their own children.

Others wrote simply to tell me about their experiences with an "Opti the Mystic" of their own and how he—or sometimes she—had shaped their game and life in a positive and lasting way.

Finally, there were those who claimed reading *Final Rounds* actually prompted them to pick up the telephone and call an aging parent and propose a golf sojourn of their own before time ran out. In a few of these cases, the estrangement had been significant, sometimes years in length.

I'll never forget the Baltimore man who wrote me that he finished the book one day and drove to see his ninety-one-year-old father in New Jersey the next. Owing to some "silly private family matter that really didn't mean anything," the two had not spoken in almost five years. Six weeks after their reunion, the pair set off for a week together in Ireland, sticks in tow. A few weeks after they returned, the father suddenly passed away. "I have tears in my eyes as I write this to you," the aging son concluded. "But that trip to Ireland was the most meaningful time we ever had together. So thanks."

Not surprisingly, I had tears in my eyes as I read the letter—and tried to think what I could possibly write back to him.

I settled for a simple thank-you of my own.

*

Which brings me to Steve Friedman's story.

Driving Lessons is the moving tale of a gifted middle-aged writer who decides, on the shoals of fifty, to go home to St. Louis to try and reconnect with an aging papa who simply adores the game of golf and wishes his son shared his passion. Like my own father, Steve's dad is an upbeat and cheerful salesman for the virtues of a game Steve never had much desire to play—until now.

Driven by the internal clock that governs all our waking days and sleepless nights, Steve Friedman goes in quest of forging something new from the ancient game of golf: a deeper and perhaps truer understanding of his father.

Among golf teachers it's a fairly common belief that learning to drive a golf ball straight and true is a difficult enterprise for a kid to master—but nigh impossible for someone attempting to learn the game in middle age. At the risk of sounding like my father's son, what Steve accomplishes and learns as he struggles to master his own demons and come to grips with the impossible physics of a game he never learned to love will both touch your heart and perhaps prompt you to consider your own spiritual loose ends and vanishing mortality.

"Enjoy the game—it ends far too soon," Opti the Mystic used to regularly tell me, back when I rarely gave two seconds of thought to his goofy, upbeat pronouncements.

Oh, that I had a chance to go back and play just one more round with my old man. Even a match against Rick and Robert would be great.

Hell, I'd even buy the beer.

CHAPTER ONE

Okay

M‍Y father tells me to grip the seven-iron "like you're holding a bird in your hands and you don't want to crush it," and I say "okay," which is what I always say to my father when I think he is criticizing me, or when I have absolutely no idea what he's talking about, or when I'm filled with a vague and guilty rage toward him, or when all three are happening at once. I say "okay" when he talks about investment strategies and tax shelters and the enduring value of discipline and why I should buckle down and write a bestseller and when he tells me the story

STEVE FRIEDMAN

of the ant and the grasshopper, which he started telling me when I was two years old. I'm forty-nine now, and I've been saying "okay" for forty-seven years.

"You want to sit, not bend," he says after I slice one.

"Okay," I say.

"Both hands working together now," he says. "Belly button focus."

I hook one.

"Uh-huh. Okay."

"Keep your lower body still."

I swing with savage intent and miss.

"Okay."

"But not completely still."

Another whiff.

"Oh, I see now. Okay. Yeah. Okay."

We face each other, holding clubs, alone together on a Tuesday afternoon at a driving range. It is a brilliant, sunny spring day in St. Louis, home of my father, and of his father's father, and—after he'd emigrated from Hungary—my father's father's father. I have come here from New York City, where I moved to twelve years ago, because my father has agreed to teach me to play golf.

I asked to golf with him because I wanted to understand his life better, because I wanted to find out what he was doing all those Wednesday afternoons and Saturday mornings and Sunday summer evenings, whether golf was a cause or a symptom of his failed marriage to my mother. I asked because I wanted to learn what my father found in the fairways and on the greens that he didn't find at home, or at work, and whether he was still looking for it.

After he'd agreed, I put off the trip for five years. Because I was busy. Because I wasn't sure I wanted to know the answers to my questions. Because neither my father nor I had ever discovered much joy in our teacher-pupil sessions, whether they involved cutting grass or changing oil or polishing shoes. And then my father had emergency bypass surgery and a subsequent bout of mild depression, and shortly after that his parents fell ill and died. I helped write the eulogies that my father delivered. And so, filled with a sense of loss and impending mortality—his and mine—I called to finalize the details of the golf lessons.

There would be three days of lessons, he said, at least a few hours a day and maybe more, culminating in a nine-hole match in which we would be joined by my older brother, who was flying in for business. Okay, I said.

He told me to read Harvey Penick's *Little Red Book.* He told me to buy or borrow a couple of irons and go to the driving range and work on my swing. He told me to practice, especially the short game, "because if you really want to play golf, if you're serious about this, that's what you do, you practice the short game."

What I heard was, "You don't really want to play golf. You're not serious. You're not serious about the short game, not serious about making money, not serious about getting married and having children, and not serious about making a success of yourself."

"Okay," I'd said, half a country away. "Okay, okay, okay."

And now, hour four of day one, I'm hooking and slicing and whiffing and topping in St. Louis. If I'd read a solitary page of Penick's book, would I be wiser? If I'd made a single trip to a driving range in New York, would I be better? If I'd done my homework, would either of us be happier? Does my father sense how I have already failed him?

"We're going to work on the fundamentals this week," my father says. "Stance, grip, putting, the short game, and the basic swing."

"Okay," I hiss, and when I look up, he is frowning, in pain, as if he knows what my *okays* really mean. I think he does know. I hate when he worries about me. I like it, too. I think he has been worrying about me for a long time.

"But most important," he says, "is that we're going to teach you to have fun. That's the most important thing."

He tries so hard. He worries so much. I want to reassure him. I want to make him proud. I want to promise that I will practice the short game and hold my club like an endangered bird, that we will stride down lush fairways together for many years to come.

But I don't, of course. I can't.

"Okay," I say.

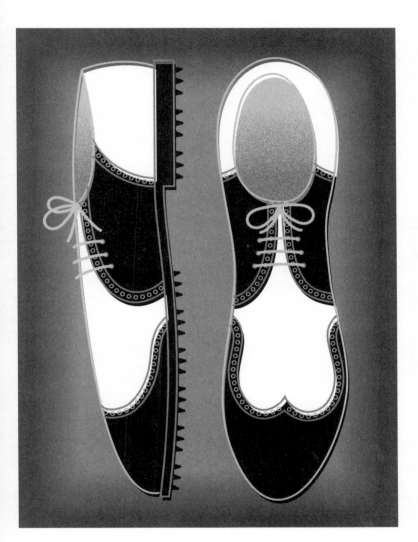

CHAPTER TWO

The Value of a Dollar

I<small>F</small> I'm a good boy when my father is playing golf on Saturday morning and I don't fight with my older brother, our mother says she'll buy us chocolate cupcakes. I'm four years old and Donnie is six, and sometimes our love of sweets overwhelms our relentless and savage rivalry. We walk together from our apartment to Platt's Delicatessen, where our mother orders a nice piece of fish. In the basement of Platt's hang the hot furs that Donnie and I have heard our parents whisper about.

Across the street from Platt's is Kranson's Drugstore, where Mr. Kranson lets me come behind the counter and sit on the dusty wooden floor and look at comic books as long as I want and as long as I don't break anything. Sometimes he even gives me a grape soda and asks how my pretty mother is doing and if my dad is still so handsome. Kranson's is where my mother sends me to get her packs of Kent cigarettes. I'm not a baby anymore, so I can walk to Kranson's by myself. A couple blocks away is Angelo's barbershop, where our father takes me and Donnie on Saturdays sometimes after he plays golf, and Donnie gets a crew cut and I get a Princeton, and afterwards we each get to buy some baseball cards at Pete's Hobby Shop next door, and after that, especially if our father had fun at golf, he takes us to Velvet Freeze for ice cream cones, chocolate for Donnie, vanilla for me, Heavenly Hash for him, and I ask if we can all play catch later. Donnie says I can't even throw right, to stop bothering Dad. "Boys," our father says, especially if he didn't have fun at golf, and we know to be quiet.

Sometimes if our father's late from golf, our mother stands at the kitchen sink and looks out the window and makes angry noises with the pots and pans while Donnie and I scoot closer to the television in the den, trying to hear Yogi and Boo Boo over the banging. But we know not to ask what's wrong, because it's better the pots and pans get it than us.

One night after dinner, when Donnie is catching fireflies, which means it's summer, I ask if I can have money to go to Kranson's to buy some comic books, please, please, PLEASE, and my father's jaw muscles move a little, which means he's mad. But my mother says, "Barry," and he says, "Okay," and she gives me four quarters. When I'm running out the door I hear my father say, "Keep it up, he'll never know the value of a dollar." That's stupid, because I know that I can buy eight twelve-cent comic books and have four cents left over for gum, or I can buy two giant-size comic books for a quarter apiece and four regular comic books and two gums, or I can get four giant-size comic books with no gum, which is what I do. I ask my father when I get home who he thinks would win in a fight, Flash or Green Lantern, and he says he doesn't know, and he sounds mean and I think I was bad but my mother says, "Who do you think would

win, Stevie?" and I say Green Lantern, if he got Flash
when Flash was sleeping, which makes my father laugh—
but I'm not being funny.

CHAPTER THREE

The Ant, the Grasshopper, and Nicole Kidman

I swing and miss. I slice one. I hook another. Four grounders. My father says nothing, and the silence is almost as awful as his advice. I am the disappointing ant. Or is it the grasshopper who couldn't get his life together? I never could keep the cautionary insects straight. I'm certain that vexed my father. It doubtless still does.

"Are you still liking New York?" he asks.

I don't mention how lonely I am, or that the Pakistani guy at the deli across the street recognizes my voice when I call for ice cream at midnight, and says, "Ah, apartment 40-F, Chubby Hubby, am I right?"

"There's always lots of stuff going on," I say.

"That's great," he says, and sends a towering drive at least 250 yards.

"Are you still saving money? Is the writing going well?"

"Oh, yeah. Great. All great."

I don't mention that my savings account is nearly depleted or that one of my recent assignments involved an online horoscope column that, when I learned how labor intensive it was to actually research planetary movements, I simply made up.

And my social life? Was I still going with Mary Frances?

I don't mention that Mary Frances, who dumped me a month earlier, had recently told me to stop e-mailing her.

"Or are you playing the field?"

He always puts the rosiest spin possible on my life. I think he's worried that if he gives a name to his concerns, they will become more real.

Yep, playing the field. Nothing serious. Just having fun. I whiff. Why can't I hit this stupid ball?

And did I remember to buy renter's insurance? And disability insurance?

Of course, I say. Yep. Lies.

"It's important, you know. Because you never know what's going to happen. You want to be protected."

Now I remember. It was the grasshopper. The grasshopper fiddled while the ant hoarded whatever ants hoard. For a long time I thought it was nuts, until I was old enough to realize that an ant had no teeth, couldn't possibly chew a nut. Before that epiphany, I was concerned mostly with the music. I wanted to know what song the grasshopper was playing and my father would sigh and tell me the song wasn't the point, it didn't matter what song the grasshopper was playing and I would nod and ask again, was it a fast song, or a sad song, or a silly song like the one about Yogi Bear, and my dad's jaw muscles would move, and then my mother would pull my head till it was touching her hip and tell my father that I just had an active imagination, and he would say it's tough to make a living with an active imagination. After that I had to go up to my room so they could have a grown-up conversation and then my mother would slam the door because she was going to "go for a drive," which is what she did when she was mad.

"Yep," I say, hacking some more, slicing, hooking, grunting, doing everything but hitting a shot that a sentient being might call a drive. Slouching toward fifty, I am an imaginative, overweight, underearning grasshopper.

"You're living the life," my father tells me. Does he really think so?

"Living the life." I am trying to believe it, trying to hit a straight drive. Failing at both.

That's when my father tells me I should invite Nicole Kidman out for a date.

"What?"

"You should ask Nicole Kidman out. She's single and she spends time in New York City sometimes."

"Great idea, Dad. I'm sure that would work." For the first time this trip, I'm smiling. Even a sad, middle-aged grasshopper appreciates the humor in florid delusion.

"No, seriously. You should. I saw in *USA Today* how she was reading that book you had an essay in. You should call her."

He has so much confidence—in himself, in his son, in the rewards of confidence. I wish I had that confidence. I'm sure he wishes it, too.

CHAPTER FOUR

Sugar

"Sugar!" I shout. "Pound for pound, pound for pound!" I don't know what "pound for pound" means, but my father says it whenever he talks about Sugar, so it's a good thing.

Sugar is my father's favorite. He likes watching boxing almost as much as he likes playing golf. He watches boxing at a place called Tony's, which is downtown, close to his office, with his friends Howard and Buddy and Uncle Teddy (who's not really our uncle but we can call him that) and that good-looking Gentile Jack, who lives between us and Kranson's. Jack could sell ice to an Eskimo, which sounds weird but Dad laughs when he says it so it's okay; Jack wears sharkskin suits, too, which sound scary but not so bad when Dad says it. I think *Gentile* means horse guy, because Dad says Jack loves the horses. Dad and Jack and Uncle Teddy play golf together and poker every Thursday night, and they talk about people named Zale and Johansson and Marciano, but Dad likes Sugar best.

Dad teaches me boxing one Sunday morning. He teaches me to keep my gloves up and to jab because those are both very important. I'm wearing big red gloves and so is Donnie. I'm five, he's seven, and we're both barefoot and have our shirts off. We're in the living room, and Dad moves the coffee table. There are white splotches on the carpet underneath its legs. I'm getting boxing lessons because our mother said she was sick and tired of Donnie and me hitting each other all the time, and when our father said boys will be boys, she slammed the door and said she was going for a drive.

Later I learned that she called Dr. Boles, who was skinny and smoked cigarettes and looked down my mouth when I was sick, and Dr. Boles said to get the boys boxing gloves.

"Sugar!" I yell, jumping and hopping, keeping my gloves up. "Pound for pound!"

I don't remember much from before the boxing match besides Kranson's and Angelo's and Velvet Freeze and comic books. I remember the ant and the grasshopper but I don't remember my dead little brother who happened when I was almost three. He was "stillborn," Donnie says, and that's a really scary word and it makes me cry. Mom lies on the couch for a long time after the stillborn baby and doesn't talk, or even eat, and we have to be quiet in the house and not yell. We get in trouble from Dad when we make noise because Mom needs to rest, she needs to get better. She cries a lot, for a long time, and we're not supposed to bother her, even if we're hungry; we should ask Cordelia, our maid, if we need anything. Cordelia is fat and lets us sit in her lap, which she didn't used to do before the stillborn baby, and Cordelia smells like the ironing board in the basement.

But now Mom is better, and we have boxing gloves. Boxing is not like wrestling because with wrestling, we get to climb on Dad and he always pretends he's about to lose before he closes his eyes and says, "I wish you boys didn't make me do this, but now I'm going to have to give you the Egyptian Bone Crusher!" and we both holler, and then he's tickling us both and I can feel how scratchy his cheeks are. But this is boxing and Dad's the ref, and it's just Donnie and me against each other.

"Pound for pound," I say. "Pound for pound. I'm Sugar!" I jab. I know what a jab is, and I am very proud of that. "Jab," I say. "Jab," I say. Donnie stands still, crew-cutted, glowering, silent. I'm not sure how long I dance and jab and call myself Sugar, but it's long enough to get tired, to stop for breath, to lower my gloves and pant. That's when Donnie clubs me on the head and I fall to the living room floor, sobbing.

"Mom!" I wail.

"Baby," Donnie says, and clubs me again.

"Boys," Dad says, holding Donnie back with one hand, tilting my chin up with the other, looking in my eyes like Dr. Boles looks when I'm sick. "Touch gloves, now. That was a good match. You both did great. You're real fighters."

I can't stop sobbing.

"It's okay, Sugar," my father says, bending down to lift me, and I can see that he is trying to stop a smile, which makes me mad, so I punch him in the neck.

Really Serious

O_{UR} second day at the range, I hit one straight and true.

"That's great!" my father says. "That's really, really great."

It's as if I've announced plans to marry, get a business degree, and move back to the Midwest, all at once.

"Now try it again. Just do the same thing again."

A capital idea, except that I, of course, have no idea what I just did. Consequently, I slice one, then hook two, then whiff, then slice four in a row.

"You're getting it," my father says, with transparent

dishonesty. "Let your hands move from eleven o'clock to one o'clock." I've never understood the clock designations for direction. "And swing from the inside out." He might as well be speaking Uzbek.

"Yep, okay," I say.

I'm a good athlete, but I've never been a quick study at sports that require balance. What I possess is a dumb, mulish capacity to absorb pain and humiliation until I master a physical movement. I remember the moment on my snowboard when I felt balanced, when a mountain of certain doom morphed into my own snowy playground; the chilly afternoon when I realized I could rock from one foot to another on my inline skates without falling. With golf, though, my straight shot seems to have nothing to do with any choices I have made. It precedes only hours of anguish.

The afternoon drags on, me screwing up nine of every ten shots, my father offering encouragement I'm sure is criticism. He mentions every few minutes that people "who are serious" about learning to play golf work on their short game. He says that people who "really want to play golf" practice a lot. If you're "serious" and "really want to play golf," you visualize great shots; you believe in yourself; you learn to play as a kid. He says this. "The great players, the ones who are really serious, who really want to become the best, they learn to play as kids."

What does that make me?

"Okay," I mutter through clenched teeth, slicing and hooking and whiffing. "Okay, okay, okay."

Then I hit another one straight and true. I can't believe it.

"You're a natural, Steve!" my father exclaims. "You're really getting this."

CHAPTER SIX

Ten Minutes

O<small>N</small> the way home from the range, my father suggests we stop for coffee. I think he senses how miserable I am. "How about Starbocks?" he says, which makes me grind my teeth. Does he mispronounce words intentionally? Where did he ever come up with "bocks"? Why am I such a bad son?

We roll onto one of the superhighways that roam the hills and floodplains of suburban St. Louis, the endless swaths of pavement that stretch to the horizon every way you look. I have always possessed a terrible sense of direction, and in the past decade St. Louis has become more confusing than ever to me. I ask how far we will be going.

"Ten minutes," he says, which makes me clench and unclench my fists. Ever since I was a child, prone to car sickness and embarrassing vomiting episodes, I would ask my father how long before we arrived at our destination. I wanted facts, exact times. I longed for the reassurance of certitude. But he offered me the same demonstrably dishonest pabulum. Two blocks, fifty miles, three state lines, it mattered not: "We'll be there in ten minutes."

He had been so looking forward to my visit. His wife—he recently remarried—is off seeing her children and grandchildren in California. Sharon is a kind woman, acutely aware of how my father yearns to connect with his grown children, and I suspect she arranged the trip for that reason. "So it'll be just you and me," he told me on the phone one evening (after suggesting reading lists and practice regimens). "We'll golf and see some movies and go out to dinner. We'll catch up. We'll have a good time."

And here I am, rocking myself in the passenger seat of his car, grinding my teeth and clenching my fists, a carsick seven-year-old in a forty-nine-year-old body. A body that isn't serious. A body that doesn't really want to learn his father's game.

CHAPTER SEVEN

Big Boy

M<small>Y</small> father and I are walking in a parking lot, and from time to time I reach out to feel his thigh. I'm nine years old. He tells me that next month he is going on a weekend trip with some of his friends to Illinois to play golf, and he says I'm a big boy now and I can keep a secret and not to tell Mommy, he's going to surprise her. Okay, I say, and I touch his thigh again, which is knotty with muscles. It's a big parking lot. I'm a worried child and I blow saliva bubbles to pass the time and to calm myself, and I am fiercely concentrating on blowing a big one as we walk and I reach out again to touch my father's thigh and then I hear a strange voice and something is wrong and I look up and it's a strange man, and then I'm sobbing and here comes my father, laughing, rubbing my head, picking me up in his arms. Somehow I have wandered off, lost in my head, but never out of sight of my father, who has watched his dreamy boy with—what? Amusement? Bafflement? Fear for the future? I bury my face in his neck and his hand covers my entire head.

When we get home, I run into the kitchen. "Mommy," I sing, "Daddy's going to Illinois to play golf with his friends." Betrayal as casual and effortless as sneaking a cookie before dinner. I don't know why I did it.

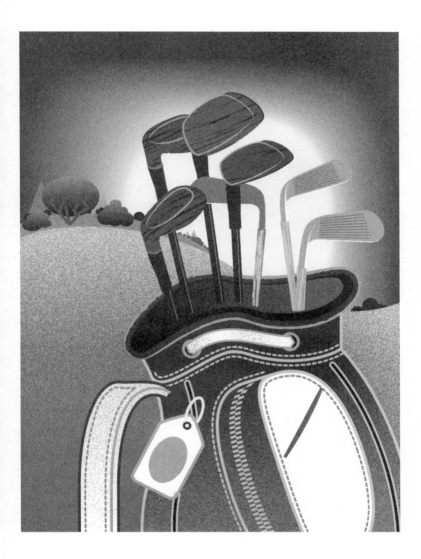

CHAPTER EIGHT

The Launcher

Our first practice session, I spotted the bulbous oblong poking out of my father's golf bag and asked about it. That was one of his drivers, he said, the Cleveland Launcher, but it would be awhile before it came out of the bag, because people who were serious about golf worked on their short game.

I have always been something of a magpie, attracted to shiny things and quick fixes.

"Okay," I said, then added that I thought I understood

the short game. I told him that I had a strong feeling that I could really hit it straight with the Launcher.

"I know a guy who changes clubs like I change underwear," my father told me. "It doesn't help his game any."

Well, sure, I said. Okay. Nevertheless, I told him, I thought the graphite technology might suit my stroke. I have no idea what graphite technology is, but I would have said anything to get my hands on the Launcher.

"It's not the driver," he said. "It's the guy hitting it."

Yeah, I understood. Okay. But what about all *his* gadgets? What about the time we were watching television together and an ad came on for Callaway's first Big Bertha and he called the 800 number and bought one?

"It's not the arrow," my father told me. "It's the Indian."

I have been whining for three days.

"Today," my father tells me on our third day of practice, as we stand at the driving range of Meadowbrook Country Club, "we are going to work on putting and chipping, we'll review your swing, and"—dramatic pause—"maybe we'll let you use the Launcher a few times."

I nearly yelp with joy. Because of the Launcher. And because the instruction is almost over. This is the second-to-last day of practice before our match, and my brother has flown in from Oregon to join us. Don is fifty-one now, a lawyer and businessman with a wife and child, college funds that have been gaining interest since before his wife was pregnant, and an aggressive-but-not-too-risky retirement strategy. He is as calculating and shrewd in his approach to golf as he is to life. Don, it should probably go without saying, has an excellent short game.

Don grabs a wedge and two irons and starts hitting. Before I can swing the Launcher, my father wants to try something new with me. He wants to introduce me to his Inside Out machine. It is another of the gadgets he owns, in direct violation of his arrow/Indian philosophy. Then again, he has always been a man of contradictions. He tells me to keep my feet still, to do the bird grip, to focus on my navel, then he adds, "But when you get up to hit the ball, trust your body. Don't think of anything." He stresses the supremacy of man over tools but later says, "If you're really serious about golf, you'll get fitted clubs." He stresses that lessons help any golfer, even the professional, that any golfer who "really wants to play" should be open to learning. Does he take lessons? "No, because it always screws up my game for weeks afterwards." So I shouldn't be surprised when Mr. It's-Not-the-Arrow places a thing that looks like a cross between an automatic sprinkler and a mechanical shoe-shine machine in front of me, sticks a ball underneath it, and tells me to swing.

"Inside out," he says.

Would it do either of us any good if I asked what in the world he was talking about?

I slice the ball.

"Try again," he says.

And I do. And I slice again. I try seven times and slice seven times.

"The ad says that on the seventh swing you'll be going straight and long," my father says. "Here, let me try."

While he works with the Inside Out, I slip the Launcher from the bag and smack one. I adore the heft, the soft little ping, the distance. I smack another. Meanwhile, Don experiments with irons and wedges, asks for exact distances to various flags, makes inquiries about how fast the greens are. And there we stand, a man and his two grown boys. My father mutters and curses at the

Inside Out until, like magic, on the seventh try, he clocks a magnificent parabola 260 yards, and then another and another. Don squints, adjusts his grip, chips, drives, toys with his swing, chips some more, asks people driving by in golf carts about the greens. I whale away with the Launcher, spraying balls everywhere, with lots of energy and very little direction.

CHAPTER NINE

Me and Bob Pettit

I am my mother's son. Fifteen years old, and while my father is playing golf and my brother is off somewhere he won't tell me about with his girlfriend, she takes me to the Hi-Pointe repertory movie theater, where we watch Fellini and Truffaut films, and afterward we drive to the bookstore and she buys me the latest "new wave" science fiction paperback, then we have iced tea. Sometimes she talks about men's toys and silly games but I focus on my drink. To even nod agreement, I know, would be to betray my father yet again.

I like sports and want to be good at them, but when people are watching I have trouble breathing and I sweat more than usual, which is a lot to begin with. My father tells me to relax and focus. He tells me if I visualize my success, it will come more easily. He has read this in *Psycho-Cybernetics*, by Maxwell Maltz, his favorite book. He quotes from it often. To my father, self-improvement through concentration is as immutable a truth as gravity. My mother sometimes listens as he instructs me in the rewards of determination and then later, over iced tea, she says I'm sensitive and I have a big imagination and that sports aren't that important anyway.

My father wore a letter sweater in high school. He played fullback and defensive back in football and guard in basketball and was a sprinter on the track team. I know this because I spend many hours looking through his scrapbooks, studying the stories from the *St. Louis Post-Dispatch* about the triumphs of the University City Indians, the exploits of ferocious blocker and rugged rebounder and swift 100-yard-dash man Barry Friedman.

I'm too sensitive for football, too slow for track. It's

basketball for me. It's not that I'm lacking in determination or desperate intentions. I attend basketball camps, read books on zone defenses, shoot hundreds of jump shots a day, and practice spin moves and reverse layups outside until dark. During high school team practices, I am always one of the high scorers and most clever pick-setters and bounce passers.

My game performances, though—no one writes stories about practices; no one has scrapbooks dedicated to practices—are marked by shortness of breath, slippery palms, and disastrous miscues. In ninth grade, inserted into my first game, I shoot at the wrong basket and I look up and see my father in the stands, wincing.

"You have to relax," he advises after one gasping, tragicomic game, then, in the next breath, "and concentrate. You can't be good if you don't concentrate." I nod. He frowns. My mom says it looks like I'm ready for a nice bowl of ice cream.

"If you imagine something," my father tells me, "you can make it happen." I think he is quoting from the blurb on the back of *Psycho-Cybernetics*. I sometimes doubt that

Maxwell Maltz is a real name. If I were going to change my name, I think I would choose "Buck" or "Slasher." I nod some more, with as much determination as I can fake.

For much of my worried, wheezing adolescence, I imagine myself filling suburban St. Louis hoops with hook shots and double-pump floaters, ridiculously high-arcing long-range jumpers and scowling power moves, but all that happens when the scoreboard is turned on and people fill the stands is shortness of breath and a surfeit of traveling violations and sweaty palms.

Now I'm sixteen, a junior in high school, and I have failed my father and myself. Two hours earlier, to provide the team with the atmosphere of a real game but without exposing us to its conference standing consequences, the coaches had staged a preseason scrimmage with a scoreboard and refs and fans, including my parents. My mother brought a John Updike novel.

I had been relaxed and had concentrated. I had visualized myself banking in shots from ingenious angles and swatting away opponents' most valiant but doomed efforts, recognizing, beneath their sweaty brows and above their frustrated snarls, the unmistakable glow of grudging admiration. Then the game had started and I had been whistled for three fouls in the first two minutes. Before the first half was even eight minutes old, I had amassed four traveling violations and seven fouls, two more than the number ordinarily sufficient to get a player ejected. Because we only had ten players on the entire team, though, I had to stay in. I ended up with one point and fourteen fouls.

I feel like throwing up, but I don't. I stare at the ceiling in my bedroom. I hear my mother hissing at my father. My father knocks on my door and, when I don't answer, enters my room.

I hate basketball. I hate the lies of *Psycho-Cybernetics* and my father's faith in them. Of course I hate my father.

He sits down on the bed and asks if I know the story of Bob Pettit.

Yeah, I know all about Bob Pettit, how he was cut from his freshman and sophomore teams in high school, and then made himself into one of the greatest basketball players of all time. It's a nice fairy tale, and my father has told it to me before, an achingly sad number of times.

"I don't believe that story."

Everyone progresses at his own speed, he tells me. You will, too, he says. Everything is going to turn out just fine. He says this like a recent Chinese immigrant might recite the Pledge of Allegiance. He knows the words are important, but he struggles with them.

He doesn't tell me I need to work harder, or that if I concentrate more, I'll get better, or that I should read *Psycho-Cybernetics* before I go to sleep. I should be grateful for this. I should thank him. I should value his generosity and his love. But I don't, of course. I can't even choke out an "Okay."

"Sounds simple," I say, viciously.

He rubs my left leg until I close my eyes.

CHAPTER TEN

Advice

I know he didn't intend it to wound. By the time I leave for college, though, I view his advice the way my mother regards his love for golf—naïve and misguided, selfish and hurtful. So I never take up the game, despite his invitations. And I don't take his advice, though he continues to offer it. Boy, does he continue to offer it.

I'm twenty-one, a college senior, and there is a fat brown envelope in the mailbox of the house where I live in California. I share the place with five others, and we cook together and drink beer and listen to the Grateful

Dead and play Frisbee and talk about how we will not make compromises in our adult professional lives. I had recently announced to my parents my plan to become a newspaper reporter. In the envelope is an article about the glut of journalists immediately post–Woodward and Bernstein. It is the mid-'70s, and I'm part of the glut. The article touches on saturation in the field, declining salaries, and shrinking profits at newspapers. At the top, in my father's scrawl, is a short note.

Maybe you should consider business. At least take some accounting courses.

I am almost thirty, have been fired from a newspaper job for my dissolute habits, and am now writing speeches for Southwestern Bell Telephone Company. I wear a suit and tie every day and take naps every Saturday afternoon. I suffer from insomnia and chronic stomachaches. When I receive an offer to work on a magazine, I can't recall ever being so happy. I call my father to share my joy.

"You're taking a 30 percent pay cut?" he asks.

"Uh-huh," I say.

"And there's no 401(k) at the magazine?"

"Right," I say.

"And no dental?"

"Yes, but . . . "

"I don't understand," he says. "I don't understand why you're doing this."

I'm forty-five and my father and I are sitting at a café in Colorado. For the past five years I've been scraping together a life as a freelance writer. A tongue-in-cheek advice book, a collaboration with a professional athlete, some newspaper articles, a fairly steady string of magazine assignments. I recently finished a dark first-person account of a long winter in the mountains and a brush with what used to be called a nervous breakdown. It's the most personal thing I've ever written; I just found out that a small literary magazine will publish it.

"You have a lot of talent," my father says.

"Thanks, Dad," I say. "That means a lot to me."

"No, really, I mean it. You should write a real book with all your talent."

"Thanks, Dad," I repeat. One thing we agree on is that my first two efforts weren't *real* books. "Thank you."

"No, really," he repeats. "You should really write a book. A real book. Have you thought about a book? It just seems a waste, with all your talent, not to write a book."

He is trying so hard. Was any father ever more encouraging to a son?

"Well, you know that piece I just sold to the literary magazine, about the winter and all that?"

He nods. I know he read it.

"Well, I'm thinking about expanding that into a book."

He looks at me, confused.

"Who would want to read that?"

CHAPTER ELEVEN

Steady

"Do you know what will ruin even a great golfer's game?"

Another trick question from my father. It's a query as vexing and nearly unanswerable as the riddle of the Sphinx or assessing the value of a dollar. I have had a lifetime to prepare, though.

"I think I do," I say, not least because we happen to be standing on the country club's practice putting green, our last drill before the big match tomorrow. My father— if he is to be evaluated on the basis of my success at saving money, cutting the front lawn, or changing the oil in my unfortunate and blameless Buick Skylark—has not been a terribly effective teacher. But he is a determined one. Even though it chafes, I admire him for that. I'm not sure what I would do if he gave up.

"And do you know what can give even a mediocre golfer a respectable score?"

"I'm going to take a wild guess and say it's putting."

He smiles wistfully at his comic book–loving boy who should be dating Nicole Kidman.

"Very good. Putting. Exactly."

He is standing eight feet from the hole, a safe, peda-gogically sensible distance from which to demonstrate the fundamentals of this important skill. I watch from the edge of the green, at least 100 feet from the hole, my putter stretched horizontally over my head, bending from my waist and grunting, trying to make my brother laugh. Don crouches, studying the surface of the green.

"Now," my father says, lining up over his ball, "the secret of putting is to keep your head down, and your eye on the ball, and to be steady, and . . . " He taps the ball into the hole, "that is how you putt."

"Or," I shout, waving my putter from above my head

with one hand, like a matador, before whacking my ball across the green, "you can just trust the force, like Yoda, and be one with the ball!" I miss by fifteen feet and my ball skitters off the green.

"That's one way to do it," Don snickers, standing, then holing his shot from ten feet, heading back to the driving range to work on different irons and, as far as I know, to experiment with different swings based on expected wind velocity, humidity levels, and fluctuating barometric pressure, which he has doubtless charted on his computer before we drove here. My dad says nothing, but I think I see his shoulders slump.

It's at that moment one of his country club pals walks onto the green. Thankfully, he hasn't witnessed my blasphemous putt. My father motions for me to join them.

"Is this your writer son?" the man asks.

"Yep, this is Steve, he lives in New York City. He used to be editor of *GQ*."

"Actually, I was *an* editor there."

"That sounds like a big job," the man says.

"It was a very big job," my father says. "Very important."

"And what are you working on now?" the man asks.

"Um." Lying to my father is one thing. Doing so to a stranger isn't quite as easy. "Um."

"One of Steve's books was a bestseller," my father says, "and now he's writing mostly magazine stories."

"Uh-huh," the man says.

"And they're really great. I'm biased, but they're really great."

That's when I decide that I will not screw around during our match. The feckless grasshopper is going to take a short vacation. I will keep my head down and my breathing steady. I will be determined. Henceforth, my father's pupil will be a dutiful, obedient, and steady golfing ant.

CHAPTER TWELVE

Magic

Driving back to my father's house we discuss the St. Louis baseball Cardinals and the football Rams. I tell him I'm playing in another basketball league and he warns me to be careful, to remember to take ibuprofen and to ice my knees, and is it really a good idea at my age, is it really worth it to play? Before I can answer he wants to know how my team is doing and what are our playoff chances? Can I still hit the turnaround jump shot? (Whether it was his Bob Pettit talk or the patience of my coach, I eventually earned a starting job on my high school team, averaged double figures on a good squad, and turned myself into a college gym rat and then a rec league terror, even when people were watching.)

He tells me he has joined an over-fifty-five softball league (he's seventy-four), and in his first game out he went 5-for-5. I tell him to be careful, to stretch before trying to leg out any doubles, not to try anything crazy. Before he can reply, I ask if he had any RBIs. He taps a beat on the steering wheel with his fingers and he honks warnings at cars idling at intersections and nosing from driveways, which annoys me. Sometimes he forgets to turn off his turn signal, and that *really* annoys me, until I realize it's not annoyance but fear. Fear that my father is showing the signs of helplessness I have always struggled to hide.

"Have you ever thought," he asks, "just to see if you could do it, not to be creative or anything, to sit down and spend some time and write a blockbuster that makes lots of money?"

While I'm grinding my teeth, he asks if I'd like to take a drive through the old neighborhood.

We drive past Kranson's, which is boarded up, and

Platt's, which is now "Discovering Optics," and past the home of Jack the horse lover, who died of a heart attack nearly forty years ago. Velvet Freeze has turned into a Greek restaurant called Momo's, Angelo's is closed, and there's a sign on Pete's Hobby Shop announcing that it's a "Snack-a-Matic."

My father taps his wheel, whistles a cheerful tune. I am near tears.

Brass bands make him smile. Nirvana is nine holes, a nice tongue sandwich, then a few hours strolling through a street fair. When he reads something in the *St. Louis Post-Dispatch* that offends his sense of rightness, he writes a letter to his congressman and is confident that it will make a difference.

He stops whistling. "One good thing about your mother . . ."

"Huh?"

"I said, one good thing about your mother, she never gave me a hard time about playing golf on Saturdays."

"*What?!?* She hated you playing golf."

"No. I don't remember that."

I can still see her glaring out the kitchen window. I

can still hear her, working over those poor, defenseless pots and pans, muttering venomously about good money and men's toys. I couldn't have imagined that. Could I? And if so, could I have been mistaken about my father's tales of ants and grasshoppers, wounded birds, and serious young men who knew the value of a dollar? Is it possible they weren't coded messages of censure? Or is he the one recasting history into a shape that suits him?

We drive past the sunken green oblong of the University City High School track. He slows, pulls over, and beams. "I used to run here," he says. "I loved those days."

I ask if he has any advice for me other than the wounded bird grip.

No. "One thing I've learned as I've gotten older is to not give advice so much. I'm trying to be more accepting, less judgmental."

I promise that I won't take any wisdom he has to offer as criticism, and he gives me a look. He knows exactly how I take his wisdom.

C'mon! What has he learned that he wants to pass on to his second son? Besides the relax-and-concentrate stuff?

"Have friends and keep them. Friends are important.

Friends make things better and they help you through tough times."

I had expected a lecture about life insurance and income flow. I should be delirious.

"Okay," I say. "Sounds good." What is *wrong* with me?

"And if you get married, or even move in with your girlfriend, make sure she's got a sense of humor. A sense of humor is important."

"That makes sense. Speaking of which, have I told you the one about the rabbi, the priest, and the imam playing golf?"

He chuckles, even though he's heard me tell it a number of times. We both tell long, corny jokes, which inspire bouts of hilarity mainly in small children and each other. We're both excellent whistlers, too, only my vibrato is better. We're each handy with a yo-yo, but while he long ago mastered the fiendish Rock the Baby, I can barely Walk the Dog. I read the sports section first, like him. We each get the same rash on our faces in times of stress or during vigorous exercise. We both incline toward get-rich-quick schemes. (My latest involves Segway tours for senior citizens in national parks; he has mused aloud about starting a publishing company that produces comic book versions of classic writers such as Shakespeare, Dostoyevsky, and Hemingway targeted at youngsters who struggle with reading comprehension.) I tuck my pants in the way I learned from watching him—underwear first, then shirttail between legs, then pull up your pants and zip. I sleep with three pillows: one hard, then one soft, and then the softest covering my eyes but not my nose, for comfort and darkness, just like my father. We both know exactly three card tricks.

*

I ask if he has any regrets. I know this sounds morose, but it's not. Winter is over and the sun is shining. We're trying our best.

"No. I've done pretty well. I'm pretty happy with the way things have turned out." He pauses. "But I wish I had been more encouraging to all my children. I should have been more encouraging."

"You were plenty encouraging, Dad." (In a lifetime

of my lies, this one feels okay.) "You told me the Bob Pettit story."

"I should have done better. And I should have paid more attention to your mother when the baby was stillborn."

"What?"

"I should have done more. I didn't really do anything."

"But no one did anything. In those days no one really talked about that stuff. There wasn't a vocabulary for miscarriages."

We have never talked about the stillborn baby. And now, suddenly, I'm an expert on sex roles, cultural norms, and birthing practices of North American Midwestern Reformed Jews in the 1950s. I want to protect my father.

"Today the hospital would let Mom hold the baby," he says.

"Sometimes they even have funerals now," I reply. "I heard that."

"That was hard. I should have been better. That was hard for everybody, but especially Mom. I should have paid more attention. But we didn't do anything. Nothing was done. I should have paid more attention."

Now we're driving past the public course where he first played golf, and now we're next to the parking lot that used to be the restaurant where he took my mother when they were teenagers. I ask what flavor milk shakes they ordered. I ask what golf course was his favorite. I ask because tales of my father's youth have always soothed me. For reasons I don't entirely understand, I lean toward my father's past like moonflowers bend into the inky night. Also, when we're talking about milk shakes from bygone days, or sports, we don't have to talk about my life, which I still suspect so often disappoints him.

He tells me he didn't take up golf until he was twenty-one and that in high school "we looked down on golfers and tennis players as sissies." He says he used to throw his clubs. He tells me that once you learn the game "you can't overthink it. Seventy percent of it is between your ears." These seem to be contradictory notions, but I keep quiet. I have become pretty good at that.

He says he plays eighteen holes twice a week, three times in the summer; that he shot a 74 in 1971 and a hole in one in June of 1992, on the eighth hole at Meadowbrook Country Club, and he has the scorecard and the ball to prove both. "You have to concentrate on every shot," he says. "Not what's been or what's going to happen." This shocks me a little, as I have never thought of my father as a Buddhist. He can quote at length from Polonious's monologue to Laertes, which surprises me not at all. His favorite drink is Crown Royal with a twist. He used to harbor crushes on Elizabeth Taylor and Jean Simmons and he likes to go out for breakfast on Sundays. He still thinks tennis is "snooty" and loves golf because, among other things, "anybody can play with anybody."

I want more. I want golf stories. I want tales of the trips to Illinois. I want anything that doesn't involve judgment of me, or advice.

He has been traveling to Illinois for forty years, ever since the trip when I ratted him out to my mother. He drove with men named Hermie and Mel, Al and Jerry, Tommy and Bob. Jerry looked like Jack Nicklaus and signed autographs. Al sometimes drank too much. Bob had a 40 handicap "and a twelve-piece swing."

"So one day Bob shoots a 40 on the front nine, and he's keeping it up on the back nine. Then on the sixteenth hole, Jerry says to him, 'You're really shooting well today, Bob,' and Bob thanks him and then Jerry says, 'But you know, I noticed you're working on that little hitch at the top of your swing; if you can smooth that out, you'll really be playing great.'

"And Bob ends up with a fifteen on the next hole and a sixteen on the last hole and he curses Jerry the rest of the trip."

When my father laughs especially hard, he starts crying. He is crying now, as we roll through suburban St. Louis. It's the happiest I have been all trip. I demand more stories. My father gives me thirty-six-hole Saturdays, followed by poker games that lasted past midnight.

Were you happy then? I want to ask. Were you worried about your future? Did you obsess about what your father thought about your career choices? What I say is, "Tell me the race story."

He was forty that year and Al challenged him to a 100-yard dash. "There were fourteen guys on the balcony watching. Eddie was the starter. Al and I had a few drinks before and I won by ten yards. So Al accuses me of cheating. So I beat him again. Then everyone's laughing and he challenges Hermie and Hermie beats him. Al says, 'Goddamit, I'm going back to the room.' We don't see him till late the next morning."

In those days, the weekend cost $45, including breakfast both mornings and dinners. In those days, my father used a Walter Hagen Black Jack putter. "I used to putt sensationally with it. I won a lot of the trophies. I was pretty good back then."

*

I ask for more stories and as he tells them, I see my father as a young man, at Tony's, with his friends. It was a little bar and the men there—it was almost entirely men—loosened their ties and watched a little black-and-white television mounted in a corner, above the liquor bottles. I was probably blowing spit bubbles at home. Uncle Teddy and Buddy and Howard were young, and good-looking Gentiles in sharkskin suits roamed the earth, and—at least in my fevered imagination—while wives all over St. Louis gritted their teeth and stared at clocks and stirred noodles, my father and his good friends gathered together for Friday night communion.

Driving through St. Louis, ten minutes from any-where, I imagine him decades ago, wondering how his life will turn out, whether he'll be serious enough to get what he wants. He is joking with his friends, cheering the fight, not even thinking about how happy he is, not knowing he should treasure the feeling, that he should hoard it. He is, I hope, looking forward to a golf match the next day.

Now we're pulling into his driveway. He reaches over, pats me on the knee. Am I ready for the match tomorrow?

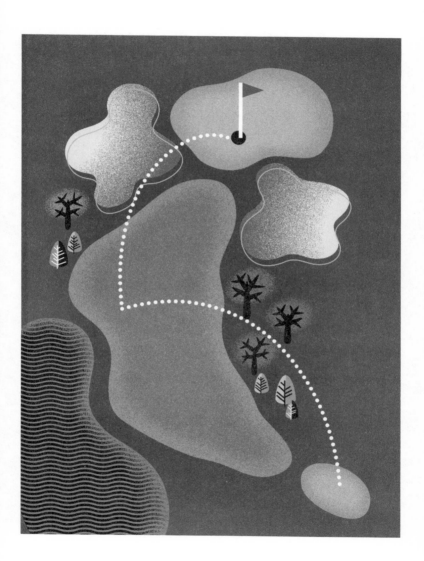

CHAPTER THIRTEEN

Keeping Score

O<small>N</small> the first tee the Launcher fails me, and I whiff. Maybe I fail myself. It's different here on the course. There are trees to worry about, and middle-aged women waiting to play behind us, and a scorecard, and my shirt keeps coming out of my shorts, which, my father tells me, is a violation of Meadowbrook Country Club policy. I try again and dribble one about ten feet. He tells me to remember about my grip, and to swing from the inside out, and to relax, to have fun, to let my body take over. I whiff again. Finally, I ground one about eighty feet.

"That's all right," my father says. "You're on the fairway. You're in good position."

"No matter how bad you are," my pragmatic older brother tells me, "if you're fast, no one will refuse to play with you."

I sprint after my ball.

It goes this way for three holes, my father and brother playing slightly above par, me hacking and whiffing and slicing and sprinting.

On the fourth hole I find myself three feet from a water hazard, then dribble three balls into it. My father reaches into his bag for his folding, snap-jawed mechanical ball retriever to snatch the balls from the pond. "Best investment I ever made," he says.

Once, Don, eyeing the green, asks whether it's 135 or 140 yards away. I tell him that even good players are a pain in the ass when they're so sluggish, and does he have to be so calculating about everything, can't he just hurry up and smack the ball? He tells me to shut up.

Once, I seven-putt. Once, I lose a ball in the woods. My father offers advice for awhile but eventually sees how it's adding to my misery.

On the seventh hole he pulls me aside.

"You know, the score doesn't matter," he says. "This is just your first time. The thing that would make me happy is if you get to like this enough that when you go back to New York, you decide to go out and play by yourself."

CHAPTER FOURTEEN

A Golf Story

In the last years of my paternal grandparents' lives, they told me a story about my father. It's a golf story. It doesn't start out that way, but trust me.

My father is three years old and his baby brother, a one-year-old whom everyone calls Sonny, is sleeping in his stroller one morning when he stops breathing. That afternoon his mother makes my father noodles and milk—his favorite—and she cries, but she doesn't say anything about why Sonny is gone, or where he is, or if he'll ever come back.

She cries for the next two years and she doesn't mention Sonny for almost seventy years after that. But my father doesn't cry.

He is sixteen years old, a high school student, a letterman, a star in football and basketball and track. He works hard. He practices. He wants to be a doctor. He is serious and really wants to do well.

He is eighteen years old, a college freshman at the University of Michigan, and it is winter break and his parents are driving him to Union Station in St. Louis, where he will board a train to return for his second semester. But he has a stomachache, he feels sick. "Let's take him home, Herman," his mother, my grandmother, says, and they do, so he can sleep and get over his stomach flu.

The next day they drive him back to the train station. But he feels sick again, so they return home. On the third day, in the car on the way to Union Station, my father feels sick once more, and his mother tells him he doesn't have to go to Michigan, he can stay home and go to school at Washington University. So he does. He goes to school in St. Louis and he gets married to his high school sweetheart and has two sons and thinks he's too old to go to medical school. He needs to support his family, so he works as a manager in the same drugstore chain as his father.

He is twenty-six and he needs more money to support his family. He tells the president of the company that if he doesn't get a raise, he will have to look for work elsewhere. The president wishes him well.

He answers a blind ad in the newspaper, an ad that calls for "smart, hardworking young men." He has a wife and two boys—the youngest of whom tends to get lost and blows saliva bubbles when he's daydreaming and throws up in the car—and a mortgage, and now he is a life-insurance salesman. He makes cold calls. Sometimes he doesn't come home until nine or ten o'clock at night. At breakfast he pores over thick booklets so he can take the test that will allow him to become a Chartered Life Underwriter. He has pens and calendars made with his name on them.

He is thirty-five years old, and now there's a third child—a five-year-old little girl—and sometimes he clenches his jaw when he's getting ready to go to work in the morning. One night when his sons can't sleep, they hear him in the kitchen cussing to their mother about the people in the head office. Sunday nights he takes his children to Steak 'n Shake for hamburgers, "to give your mom a break." On the evenings when it's the second son's turn to ride in the front seat, there is a serious speech about enjoying oneself, how it's important to relax, that there's no need to hurry into marriage, that "you have the rest of your life to be responsible." The boy is eleven years old.

At night the boy's father goes to sleep before anyone else in the house because he's so tired. On Saturday mornings, though, he wakes whistling, beaming. On Saturday mornings he plays golf. He comes home smelling of grass and grinning. He has his Saturdays, and sometimes Wednesday afternoons, and the occasional summer Sunday evening, and his annual trip to Illinois with his friends.

He returns from those trips expansive, talking about "honor" and how in golf "there's no referees, you have to trust yourself and the people you're playing with," and how "I've never met a man who cheats on the golf course who I like in life," and how "if a man plays square, you can trust him with anything." A few times he brings home a first-place trophy. "Bigger than the one in the U.S. Open," he says, laughing.

He is sixty-one, divorced, and remarried for ten years. He is more relaxed now, less worried, less tired.

He plays golf a lot, sometimes with his new wife. His children have never seen him so happy. When his wife is diagnosed with inoperable brain cancer, she insists that he keep playing golf, and he does, until her last two months, when he stays at home with her, feeding her and taking care of her in the bedroom, which she doesn't leave. When she dies, he grieves, of course, and he has some fainting spells. And then he thinks of Sonny—he hasn't thought of Sonny in decades—and for the first time he cries for his little brother and he can't stop.

Ten years pass, and he has chest pains and emergency bypass surgery and a bout with depression and a few girlfriends who don't work out. And then he meets a woman named Sharon who doesn't golf but says that if it's important to him, she'll learn.

And now he is seventy-four, married for the third time. He tells his children he loves them often, spoils his thirteen grandchildren and step-grandchildren with bicycles and computer games and toy trucks and trips to the zoo and sleepovers and ice cream sundaes in the middle of the day. Not one of them knows what a step-grandchild is. The word would mystify them. He is a lifetime member of the Million Dollar Round Table, which, in the life-insurance business, is as good as it gets. He is one of the most successful salesmen in the country, an innovator who sold the first group tax-sheltered annuity in the world.

(I know what a group tax-sheltered annuity is now. I know that it has earned his company many billions of dollars.)

"Your company should name a building after you," I say between a slice and a hook.

"They don't even know my name," he replies.

He paid for his three children's college education, offered them choices and career opportunities he might have dreamed about but could never pursue. He skis, owns property in a resort town, spends winters in Palm Springs, works when he wants, travels when he wants. All of that came to him because he was serious, because he really wanted it. Hard work and thrift and serious-ness of purpose have formed the bulwark for him against pain and loss, but they haven't been enough. Still, what else is there?

Isn't it obvious?

There are Saturdays and Wednesdays and summer Sunday evenings and a place where he can breathe fresh air and stretch and play, where honor means something and where people don't cheat.

I want to tell him how proud I am of him, how I wish I could live up to the example he set, how I envy him his discipline and success and self-sacrifice and gen-erosity. I want to tell him how much he means to me. But I can't. So I vow to do the next best thing. I will hit a good shot before our match ends. If I need to be serious, I will be serious. If I need to really want it, I will really want it. Whatever it takes, I will do it.

Anything to hit a good shot.

CHAPTER FIFTEEN

You Never Know

I don't, of course. I don't hit a good shot. If it were that easy, if striking the ball cleanly and with strength and purpose and something approaching artistry were as simple as merely distilling all the resentment and misunderstanding and rage and wounded feelings and guilt and gratitude and love a son holds toward his father into a smooth and honest and powerful swing, there would be legions of scratch golfers launching millions of elegant drives all over the world. There would be so many white dimpled balls arcing across the skies that no one would see the sun.

But it's not that easy. So I whiff and hack and sprint and goad my brother, who plays with grim cunning. I kid my father about the ball retriever and ask him to tell me more stories of the trips to Illinois, and I beg for tales from his early days in the insurance business and of his best shots and his favorite afternoons on the golf course.

I stop worrying about my grip and my stance. I relax, and I stop trying so hard, and if you're a golfer, or a father, or a son, of course you know what happens next.

I can still see it leaving the Launcher, soaring, a blur of white against the deep green of the trees, the baby blue of the Midwestern afternoon. A white smudge, low to the ground, a vector bending toward the distant green.

A mystery.

"Great shot!" my father yells. He applauds. "That's a great shot!" he yells again, and applauds some more.

"I don't know how I did it," I say as he comes over to pat me on the back.

It doesn't matter, he tells me. What's important is that I did it, and that I'm having fun.

I'm not sure if I'll go to the driving range with friends. I don't know if I'll ever pick up a club again. It doesn't matter. We walk together, up the fairway, my father and I. He will shoot a 42 for the nine holes. I will finish at 86.

We are blessed.

"That's the great thing about this game," he tells me, his arm around my shoulder. It is a mild, sunny day, and the grass is soft and springy and the Emerald City of the final hole beckons. This is the lush fairway I imagined. "Even if you have a bunch of bad shots," my father says, "you never know when you're going to hit a good one. And that good one can save you."

Acknowledgments

I thank John Atwood for sending me to St. Louis to learn golf from my father, and for helping me transform those lessons into this book. Thanks also to Shannon Welch, for her patient and thoughtful editing. For reading various drafts and suggesting improvements, I thank Ann Friedman, Don Friedman, Janet Hupert Friedman, Ken Fuson, and Jeff Leen. For his powerful example, his enduring patience, and his great love, I thank my father.